3

4

5

8

9

10

13

14

15

18

19

20

elcome to Cross Stitch for the Soul!

Hand embroidery, in all of its forms, is a beautifully calming and mindful occupation. It is a million miles away from the fast-paced and stressful lives many of us lead in today's busy world.

I rediscovered cross stitch as an adult as a bit of an escape and found it to be wonderfully meditative; a chance to embrace slowness and create something beautiful at the same time. As someone who has experienced anxiety and depression, I found the ability to switch off and stitch was hugely welcome.

The 20 designs in this collection are quotes that resonate with me for many reasons and which I have brought to life in cross stitch in my own colourful, typographic way. I hope they bring you joy, both through the stitching process and in whatever you choose to do with them once complete – be it gifting, hanging on your wall, or keeping somewhere special for days when you need a bit of a boost.

 *Emma*

CROSS STITCH for the SOUL

20 DESIGNS to inspire

EMMA · CONGDON ·

DAVID & CHARLES

www.davidandcharles.com

# Contents

1

6

7

11

12

16

17

# Tools and Materials

## Fabric

When it comes to fabric there are so many options, but my lasting love will always be for Aida. The pre-woven holes make stitching a breeze. I'm all about enjoyment when it comes to stitching and, as much as I appreciate the neatness of linen or Hardanger, the stress of working with it can override the enjoyment of stitching itself. It's important to not take on too much or work on something that you struggle with, so choose your fabric wisely.

Throughout this book I have recommended specific fabrics to use on each piece. These are chosen to work best with the colours but, of course, substitutions can always be made to suit stitching your own style. Here's a simple breakdown of the individual fabric types:

- **Aida** is an open and even weave cotton fabric. It has a natural mesh that helps guide the stitcher and enough stiffness that for smaller projects a hoop isn't always required.

- **Fiddler's Cloth** is similar to Aida but is slightly irregular, producing a more rustic, aged look, which is good if you want something a little less perfect.

- **Hardanger** is made of 100% cotton at 22-count. It is typically used for Hardanger embroidery but can also be used for cross stitch to give a much finer finish. It's trickier to work with because of its size but the results can be well worth it if you're up to the challenge.

- **Linen** has a crisp feel with a finer weave than Aida so is usually stitched over two threads of the fabric rather than one. It offers a more traditional look. Working with linen can be a bit more challenging, but is well worth the effort.

- **Jobelan** is a soft fabric with a slight sheen. It is also stitched over two threads, but is more resistant to wrinkles compared to linen. It's easy to wash, so is ideal for larger projects for the home, such as tablecloths and pillows.

## Thread

Thread is the paint of the stitching world and offers endless creative possibilities. However, with counted cross stitch it's super simple to use and the worst that can happen is that it can knot. I always recommend working with two strands for whole stitches (so dividing the original thread into three sets of two strands) and then working with lengths of around 30-50cm (12-20in), adjusting them on your needle to get started. For backstitch use a single strand.

In this book I have used DMC stranded cotton (floss), but there are many alternatives available and the conversion chart at the end of this book will help you to get the closest colour matches.

## Scissors

Good embroidery scissors are sharp and fine-pointed for cleanly cutting thread to the correct length, and for snipping off loose ends. To keep them sharp, never use them to cut paper or fabric. Instead you will need a separate pair of fabric scissors to cut your Aida or linen.

## Needles

Like most things, you can get by with needles that are too big or too small, but using a good embroidery needle that is the right size for the fabric will make stitching much quicker and easier. Tapestry needles are best for cross stitch because they have a rounded point so will not snag the fabric. However, always be careful with where they are left (please never, ever, cross stitch in bed!). A magnetic needle minder is a good idea to give you somewhere to 'park' your needle when it's not in use – there are so many fun designs available.

## Frames

Frames keep your fabric taut while working, can save you a huge amount of time and also ensure that your stitching is even. I like to keep it simple and use a bamboo hoop but there are many varieties available, including some really fancy ones that you don't even have to hold! Try out a few different models if you're unsure. A local craft store can be a good source of inspiration and advice here.

A t times, it's easy to feel dissatisfied with our lives. We focus on what we haven't achieved rather than what we have. However, positive affirmations are known to help break this negative thinking. Start with gratitude for the things you have, and set yourself up in a positive way for a new day and all the possibilities it brings with it.

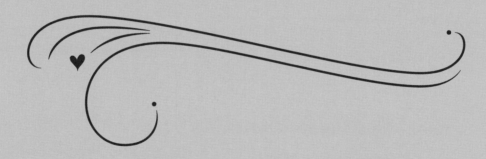

**Info**
Stitch count: 129 x 96
Stitched size (on 14-count
Aida or 28-count linen):
23.4 x 17.4cm (9¼ x 6⅞in)

**Shopping List**
· 1 skein of each DMC
  stranded cotton (floss)
  listed in the chart key

· Ivory Aida or linen, at
  least 38 x 33cm (15 x 13in)

*Model stitched by Clare Prowse & Michelle Luscombe*

DMC
Stranded
cotton

Cross Stitch

| # | 9 |
| --- | --- |
| Z | 977 |
| ↓ | 743 |
| ♥ | 744 |
| ⊠ | 3816 |
| ▽ | 3765 |
| ◪ | 3712 |
| ◐ | 967 |
| ◰ | 3854 |
| ⋈ | 834 |
| ◇ | 3813 |
| U | 3756 |
| ◣ | 604 |

Backstitch

| — | 3813 |
| — | 3765 |

he worst thing in life is to have regrets. Not doing things for fear of doing them at a slower pace than others can sometimes mean you put them off, often forever, and you miss out. But everything has to start somewhere and if you don't try it'll never happen, so don't be afraid to give it a go.

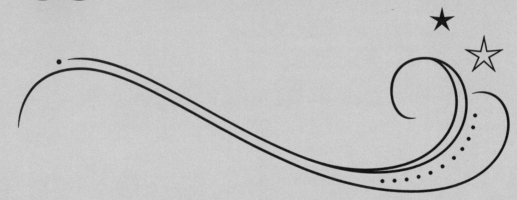

## Info
Stitch count: 117 x 186
Stitched size (on 14-count
Aida or 28-count linen):
21.2 x 33.8cm (8⅜ x 13½in)

## Shopping List
· 1 skein of each DMC
  stranded cotton (floss)
  listed in the chart key

· Ivory Aida or linen, at least
  37 x 50cm (14½ x 20in)

*Model stitched by Michelle Luscombe*

DMC Stranded cotton

Cross Stitch
➜ 818
⊠ 976
◥ 166
◐ 561
▧ 3816
◣ 3733
◼ 352
↑ 3782
▽ 581
♥ 3813
# 34

Backstitch
— 976
— 166
— 561
— 34
— 3733

- 14 -

DMC Stranded cotton

**Cross Stitch**

| | |
|---|---|
| ➜ | 818 |
| ⋈ | 976 |
| ◰ | 166 |
| ◯ | 561 |
| ▣ | 3816 |
| ◣ | 3733 |
| ◪ | 352 |
| ↑ | 3782 |
| ▽ | 581 |
| ♥ | 3813 |
| # | 34 |

**Backstitch**

| | |
|---|---|
| — | 976 |
| — | 166 |
| — | 561 |
| — | 34 |
| — | 3733 |

ife can throw you into unexpected situations that you could never have imagined or planned for, but that can be one of the most beautiful things about it. It's important, however, that you always embrace life around you rather than yearning for something else. Have dreams and goals of course, but don't let them overwhelm your ability to enjoy and flourish where you are.

**Info**
Stitch count: 129 x 96
Stitched size (on 14-count
Aida or 28-count linen):
23.4 x 17.4cm (9¼ x 6⅞in)

**Shopping List**
- 1 skein of each DMC stranded cotton (floss) listed in the chart key

- Clay or Celadon Green Aida or linen, at least 40 x 34cm (15¾ x 13½in)

*Model stitched by Sandra Doolan*

DMC
Stranded
cotton

Cross Stitch
⊙ BLANC
◣ 353
⊔ 722
· 734
→ 991
6 3840
U 604
A 351
↘ 721
◤ 869
▭ 581
3 3809
◪ 34
▤ 603

Backstitch
— 351

ife would just be dull if we were only handed the sweetest things. That's why it throws us a bitter-tasting lemony curveball every so often (or even worse, a raw onion or two). This saying is a great metaphor for how sour life situations can be made sweet with a bit of practise and creativity – not to mention a good bit of elbow grease.

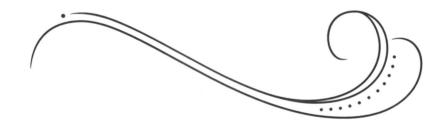

### Info
Stitch count: 98 x 130
Stitched size (on 14-count Aida or 28-count linen):
17.8cm x 23.6cm (7 x 9⅜in)

### Shopping List
- 1 skein of each DMC stranded cotton (floss) listed in the chart key

- Antique white Aida or linen, at least 33 x 38cm (13 x 15in)

*Model stitched by Eleanor Welsh*

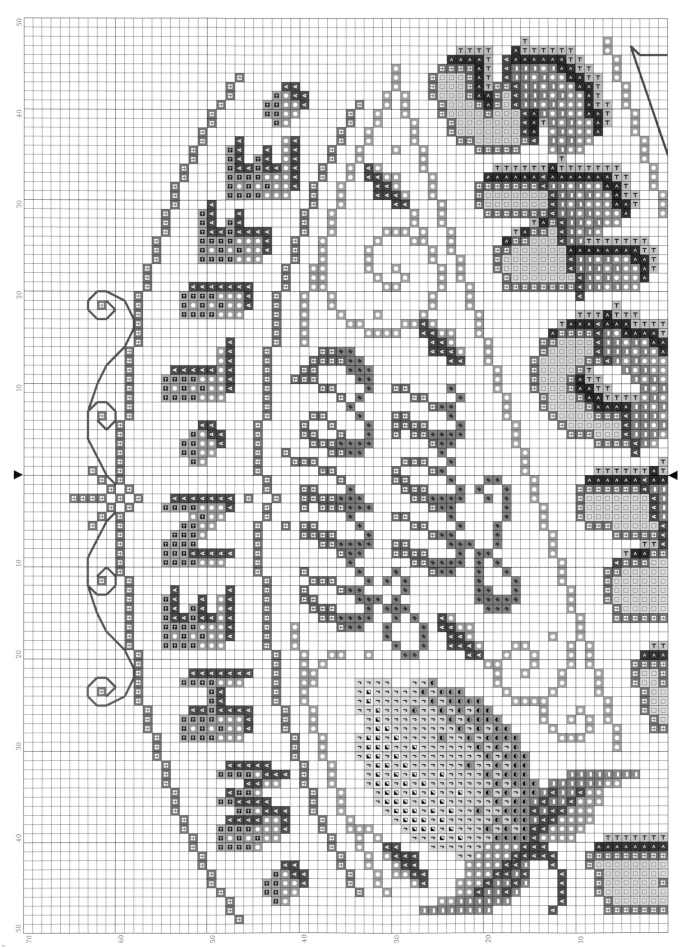

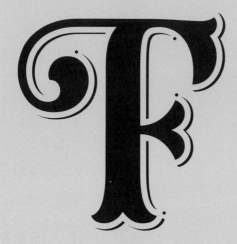

**F**ull of metaphors for life, the sea can be blissfully calm one moment, then terrifying and dangerous the next – it's everchanging. We adapt and learn to be best-equipped to face the toughest daily challenges; to know what sails to hoist to get through it in one piece (and hopefully avoid the sharks). It's what helps you to appreciate life when the sun shines again and the water is calm.

**Info**
Stitch count: 131 x 199
Stitched size (on 14-count
Aida or 28-count linen):
23.8 x 36.1cm (9½ x 14¼in)

**Shopping List**
· 1 skein of each DMC
  stranded cotton (floss)
  listed in the chart key,
  plus 1 additional skein
  of colour 3808

· Light Grey Aida or
  linen, at least 40 x 52cm
  (15¾ x 20¾in)

*Model stitched by Eleanor Welsh*

DMC
Stranded
cotton

Cross Stitch

P  351
L  712
U  747
▽  930
◑  3810
6  3844
▪  931
✕  349
◣  3821
↑  3811
=  3846
W  3808
⊙  3845
◇  3766
C  311

Backstitch
▬ 3808

DMC
Stranded
cotton

Cross Stitch

**P** 351
**L** 712
**U** 747
**V** 930
**C** 3810
**6** 3844
**■** 931
**X** 349
**L** 3821
**↑** 3811
**=** 3846
**W** 3808
**◉** 3845
**◇** 3766
**C** 311

Backstitch
**——** 3808

- 30 -

n some days everything just seems to go wrong… you miss the bus, you get caught in the rain, you drop your phone. However, even in these trying times there will be good things, I promise – they just might be harder to spot. If you look hard enough you'll be able to notice and appreciate them and put a positive spin on any day.

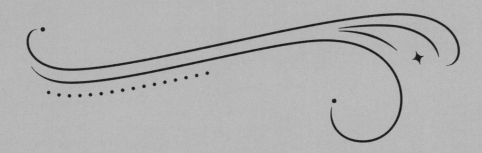

**Info**
Stitch count: 130 x 198
Stitched size (on 14-count
Aida or 28-count linen):
23.6 x 35.9cm (9⅜ x 14⅛in)

**Shopping List**
- 1 skein of each DMC stranded cotton (floss) listed in the chart key

- Antique White Aida or linen, at least 40 x 52cm (15¾ x 20¾in)

*Model stitched by Glenda Dickson*

DMC
Stranded
cotton

Cross Stitch

◤ 3340
▣ 733
◪ 470
◖ 335
▨ 3802
▭ 833
▢ 166
V 3726
⬇ 3326
E 223

Backstitch
— 921
— 833
— 3802
— 223

DMC
Stranded
cotton

Cross Stitch

| | |
|---|---|
| ◣ | 3340 |
| ▧ | 733 |
| ◣ | 470 |
| ◖ | 335 |
| ◪ | 3802 |
| ⊢ | 833 |
| ⌐ | 166 |
| V | 3726 |
| ⇩ | 3326 |
| E | 223 |

Backstitch

| | |
|---|---|
| — | 833 |
| — | 3802 |
| — | 223 |

ocial pressures, advertising and social media make it difficult for us to be content with both our internal and external selves. There's always someone skinnier, richer, or more successful to make us think less of ourselves. But wishing for a life that isn't your own is wasting the time that you have. We're all different – be proud of yourself for whatever you bring to the table.

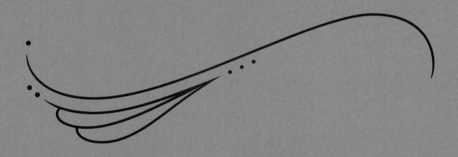

**Info**
Stitch count: 89 x 95
Stitched size (on 14-count
Aida or 28-count linen):
16.2 x 17.2cm (6⅜ x 6¾in)

**Shopping List**
· 1 skein of each DMC
stranded cotton (floss)
listed in the chart key

· Light Blue Aida or linen,
at least 32 x 33cm
(12½ x 13in)

*Model stitched by Sharon Atkinson*

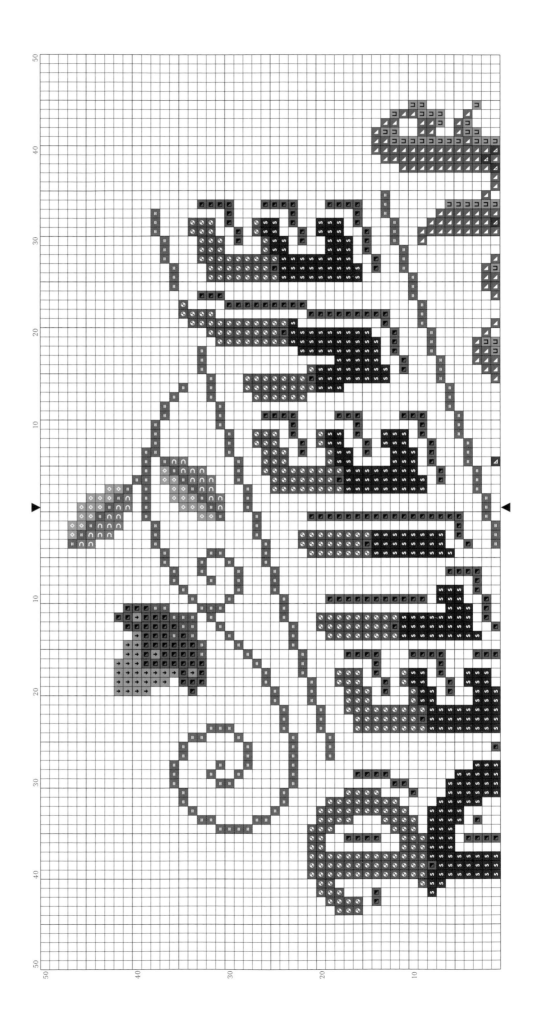

DMC
Stranded
cotton

Cross Stitch

| | |
|---|---|
| ◇ | 704 |
| = | 987 |
| ◣ | 3760 |
| ◕ | 33 |
| S | 35 |
| C | 988 |
| ⊔ | 3846 |
| ◿ | 3842 |
| ↓ | 3609 |
| ◩ | 603 |

**B**eing friendly, generous and considerate towards others – it's just *kind*. A good deed means you're not only helping someone in need, you're also giving yourself a boost knowing that you've done something selfless. It doesn't matter how big or small the gesture is, it'll give you a wonderfully rewarding feeling and put a spring in your step.

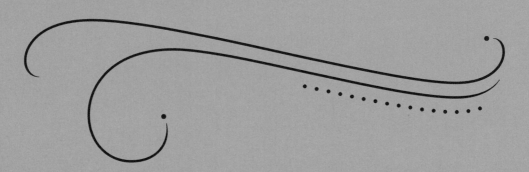

### Info
Stitch count: 100 x 124
Stitched size (on 14-count
Aida or 28-count linen):
18.1 x 22.5cm (7⅛ x 8¾in)

### Shopping List
· I skein of each DMC
  stranded cotton (floss)
  listed in the chart key

· Platinum Aida or linen,
  at least 24 x 39cm
  (9⅝ x 15¼in)

*Model stitched by Hayley Wellock*

DMC
Stranded
cotton

Cross Stitch

| Symbol | DMC |
|---|---|
| V | 351 |
| ⧓ | 720 |
| ◺ | 833 |
| = | 3047 |
| C | 3816 |
| ○ | 3772 |
| ▙ | 725 |
| ⌝ | 834 |
| ➔ | 3817 |
| ✓ | 3706 |

Backstitch

- 351
- 3064
- 833
- 3817

ature is amazing and a great source of inspiration for me. I find it magical that something so seemingly dreary as rain can produce something as beautiful as a rainbow. The same is true of the night sky. If you can escape the city, look up and appreciate the stars that aren't visible unless the sky is sufficiently dark. Finding the best in bad situations isn't easy – but worth it.

**Info**
Stitch count: 128 x 189
Stitched size (on 14-count
Aida or 28-count linen):
23.2 x 34.3cm (9⅛ x 13⅝in)

**Shopping List**
- 1 skein of each DMC stranded cotton (floss) listed in the chart key

- White Aida or linen, at least 38 x 48.3cm (15 x 19in)

*Model stitched by Nicola Gravener*

DMC
Stranded
cotton

Cross Stitch

| | |
|---|---|
| ↗ | 26 |
| Z | 312 |
| + | 318 |
| = | 333 |
| 0 | 351 |
| Ц | 728 |
| ε | 775 |
| ⫽ | 973 |
| ⊥ | 3755 |
| ⊏ | 3854 |
| ▬ | 155 |
| ↑ | 317 |
| ⋈ | 322 |
| ◣ | 336 |
| ⬦ | 554 |
| ⮊ | 762 |
| # | 906 |
| ◖ | 3746 |
| ⌐ | 3819 |

Backstitch
▬ 317

DMC
Stranded
cotton

**Cross Stitch**

| | |
|---|---|
| ⚒ | 26 |
| Z | 312 |
| ✚ | 318 |
| ▤ | 333 |
| ◉ | 351 |
| ⊔ | 728 |
| ❧ | 775 |
| ❦ | 973 |
| ⊥ | 3755 |
| ◰ | 155 |
| ↑ | 317 |
| ⋈ | 322 |
| ◣ | 336 |
| ❥ | 554 |
| ⬌ | 762 |
| # | 906 |
| ◑ | 3746 |
| ⌐ | 3819 |

**Backstitch**

| | |
|---|---|
| ▬ | 317 |

ou find that the challenging things in life feel less extreme when you're not facing them alone. Whether it's just taking the dog on a really strenuous walk, or supporting a loved one through an illness, being with ones you love in difficult situations can help you to get through them. So, keep talking, keep supporting and keep walking together.

## Info
Stitch count: 96 x 129
Stitched size (on 14-count Aida or 28-count linen): 17.4 x 23.4cm (6⅞ x 9¼in)

## Shopping List
· 1 skein of each DMC stranded cotton (floss) listed in the chart key

· Parchment Aida or linen, at least 33 x 39cm (13 x 15¼in)

*Model stitched by Clare Prowse*

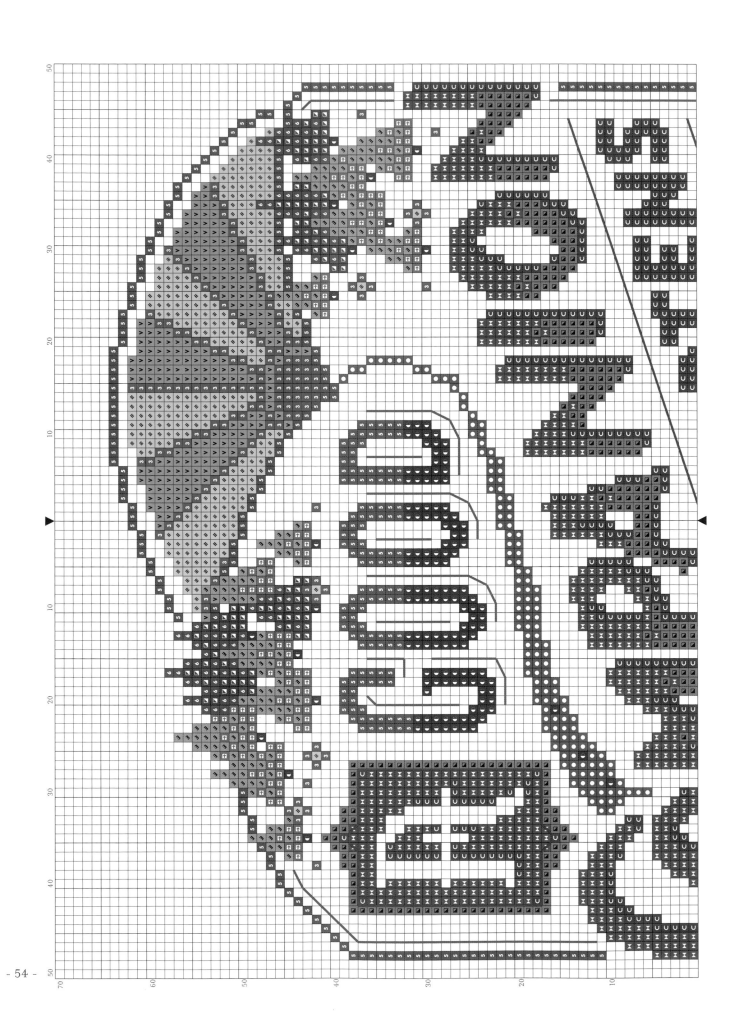

DMC
Stranded
cotton

**Cross Stitch**

| | |
|---|---|
| 5 | 3860 |
| ◐ | 433 |
| S | 3828 |
| ◪ | 730 |
| → | 470 |
| ◿ | 520 |
| ⋈ | 33 |
| V | 3825 |
| 3 | 721 |
| ◯ | 420 |
| ◈ | 3855 |
| 6 | 580 |
| ◞ | 471 |
| C | 29 |
| ◨ | 3836 |

**Backstitch**

— 3860
— 3825
— 29

Greek Proverb

ertainly, patience is a good thing to have, but the most inspirational people throughout history are always known for going one step further and really pushing themselves. Actively pursuing your personal goals can be a tremendous boost to happiness. Even if you live a good life, if there is something you've always wanted to try, don't hesitate, just do it.

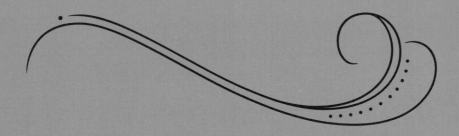

**Info**
Stitch count: 129 x 196
Stitched size (on 14-count
Aida or 28-count linen):
23.4 x 35.6cm (9¼ x 14in)

**Shopping List**
- 1 skein of each DMC stranded cotton (floss) listed in the chart key, plus 1 additional skein of colour 721

- Navy Aida or linen, at least 40 x 52cm (15¾ x 20¾in)

*Model stitched by Michelle Luscombe*

DMC
Stranded
cotton

Cross Stitch
▽ 608
⋈ 741
L 445
⋈ 747
— 3845
▽ 517
⌐ 153
◢ 3806
◯ 721
∩ 444
◣ 964
• 3846
◩ 3844
♥ B5200
◎ 3608
⊙ 604

Backstitch
— 820

DMC
Stranded
cotton

Cross Stitch

▼ 608
▷◁ 741
L 445
▷◁ 747
– 3845
▽ 517
⌐ 153
◢ 3806
○ 721
∩ 444
◢ 964
· 3846
◩ 3844
♥ B5200
◎ 3608
⊙ 604

Backstitch
▬ 820

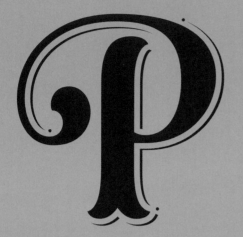

**P**retending to be someone you're not to please others can be exhausting and ultimately draining. We're all unique and have our own special gifts to give to the world, so you should never be ashamed of who you are. Those who want to be with the real you, and make you feel proud of who you are, will always agree.

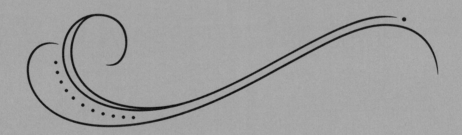

**Info**
Stitch count: 126 x 194
Stitched size (on 14-count
Aida or 28-count linen):
22.9 x 35.2cm (9 x 13⅞in)

**Shopping List**
· I skein of each DMC
  stranded cotton (floss)
  listed in the chart key

· White Aida or linen,
  at least 39 x 51cm
  (15¼ x 20⅜in)

DMC
Stranded
cotton

**Cross Stitch**

| | |
|---|---|
| ◖ | 351 |
| ▽ | 371 |
| ⊙ | 372 |
| ▼ | 803 |
| ◣ | 341 |
| ⋈ | 948 |
| ▣ | 370 |
| ━ | 794 |
| ∩ | 161 |
| ◣ | 604 |

**Backstitch**

| | |
|---|---|
| ━ | 351 |
| ━ | 371 |
| ━ | 3842 |

DMC
Stranded
cotton

Cross Stitch

C 351
▽ 371
⊙ 372
▼ 803
◣ 341
⋈ 948
⊡ 370
▬ 794
◠ 161
◥ 604

Backstitch

▬ 351
▬ 371
▬ 3842

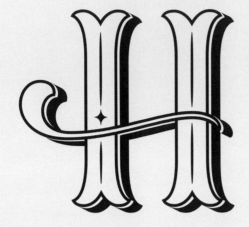 iking is much like life. There can be peaks and troughs, and it can seem perilous at times. But once you've got to the top you get a huge sense of achievement. Whatever the incline, keep taking the next step to get to your destination – you'll get there. You can proudly look back at how far you've come and appreciate that as much as the view itself.

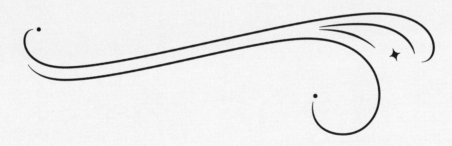

**Info**
Stitch count: 97 x 96
Stitched size (on 14-count
Aida or 28-count linen):
17.6 x 17.4cm (7 x 6⅞in)

**Shopping List**
· 1 skein of each DMC
  stranded cotton (floss)
  listed in the chart key

· White Aida or linen,
  at least 34 x 33cm
  (13½ x 13in)

*Model stitched by Clare Prowse*

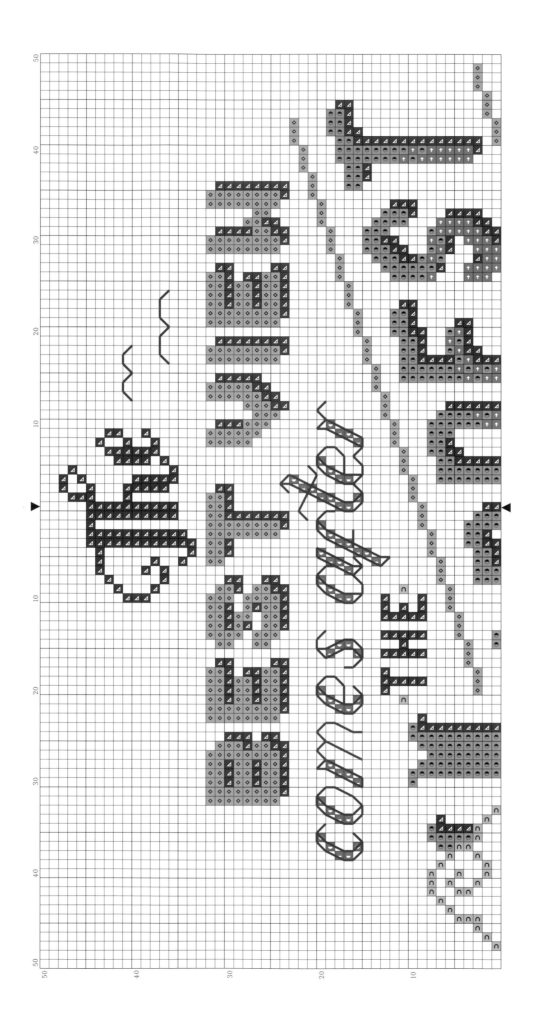

DMC Stranded cotton

Cross Stitch

| | |
|---|---|
| 5 | 869 |
| ◖ | 581 |
| ◣ | 3816 |
| ◐ | 3846 |
| ◑ | 3810 |
| W | 340 |
| 6 | 166 |
| ◇ | 3817 |
| ⊃ | 3811 |
| ◣ | 3808 |
| → | 3844 |

Backstitch

| | |
|---|---|
| ▬ | 869 |
| ▬ | 3808 |

he Bard knew his stuff. These words say it like it is. It's difficult to love the person who stole or broke something precious to you – especially your heart. But holding on to bad feelings about anyone ultimately hurts you more than it hurts them. Accept people for who they are, understand and be compassionate towards those who you don't know, and treat people the way you like to be treated yourself.

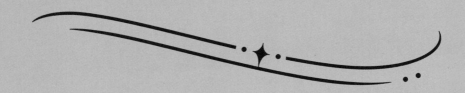

**Info**
Stitch count: 130 x 198
Stitched size (on 14-count Aida or 28-count linen): 23.6 x 35.9cm (9⅜ x 14⅛in)

**Shopping List**
- 1 skein of each DMC stranded cotton (floss) listed in the chart key

- Antique White Aida or linen, at least 40 x 52cm (15¾ x 20¾in)

*Model stitched by Glenda Dickson*

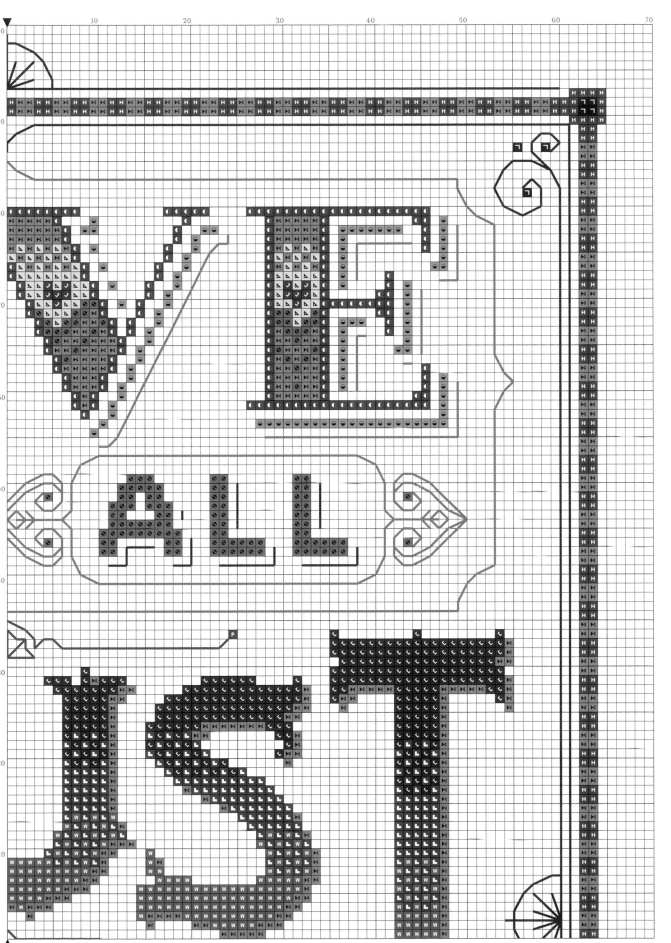

DMC
Stranded
cotton

Cross Stitch

| / | 699 |
| ⊐ | 777 |
| ↓ | 470 |
| N | 166 |
| ↘ | 350 |
| ◖ | 422 |
| ✪ | 3733 |
| ⋈ | 3354 |
| P | 3765 |
| ↰ | 158 |
| ◰ | 3807 |
| ◖ | 3731 |
| W | 3839 |
| H | 720 |
| ● | 564 |
| ↖ | 819 |

Backstitch

| ━ | 3765 |
| ━ | 777 |
| ━ | 166 |
| ━ | 899 |

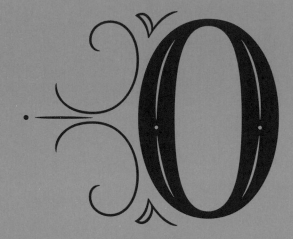 bvious to some perhaps, but it's very easy to slip into situations in work and life that are convenient but that don't bring you joy. Sadly, not all jobs are fun, but it's about getting balance. Try always to have things in your life that you enjoy – dig out that old guitar, that tennis racket, those tap shoes and your cross stitch supplies (obviously)… and do something you love.

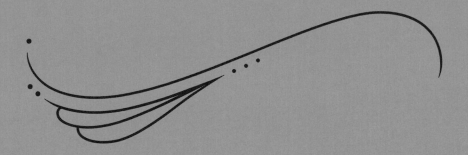

**Info**
Stitch count: 97 x 94
Stitched size (on 14-count
Aida or 28-count linen):
17.6 x 17.1cm (7 x 6¾in)

**Shopping List**
· 1 skein of each DMC
  stranded cotton (floss)
  listed in the chart key

· Navy Aida or linen,
  at least 34 x 33cm
  (13½ x 13in)

*Model stitched by Sharon Atkinson*

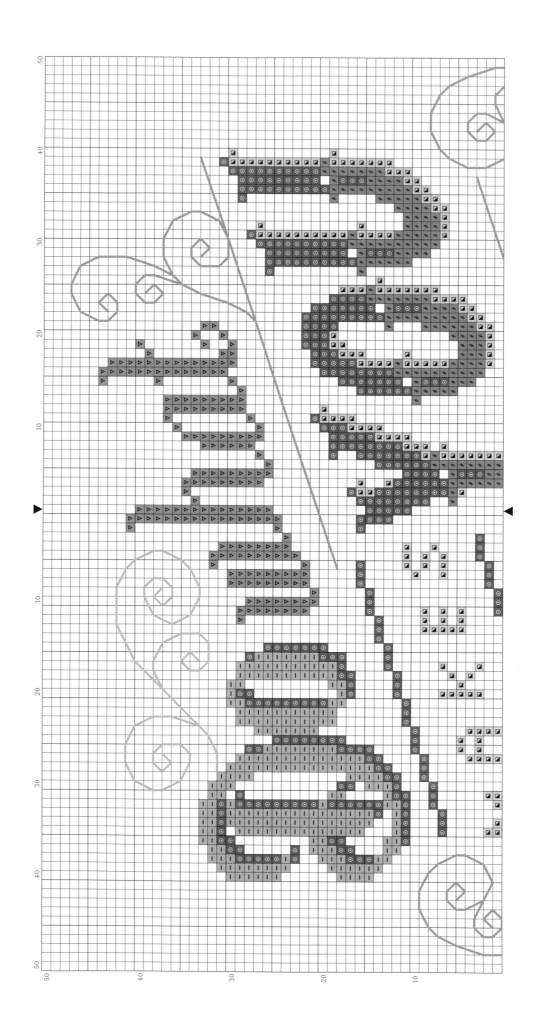

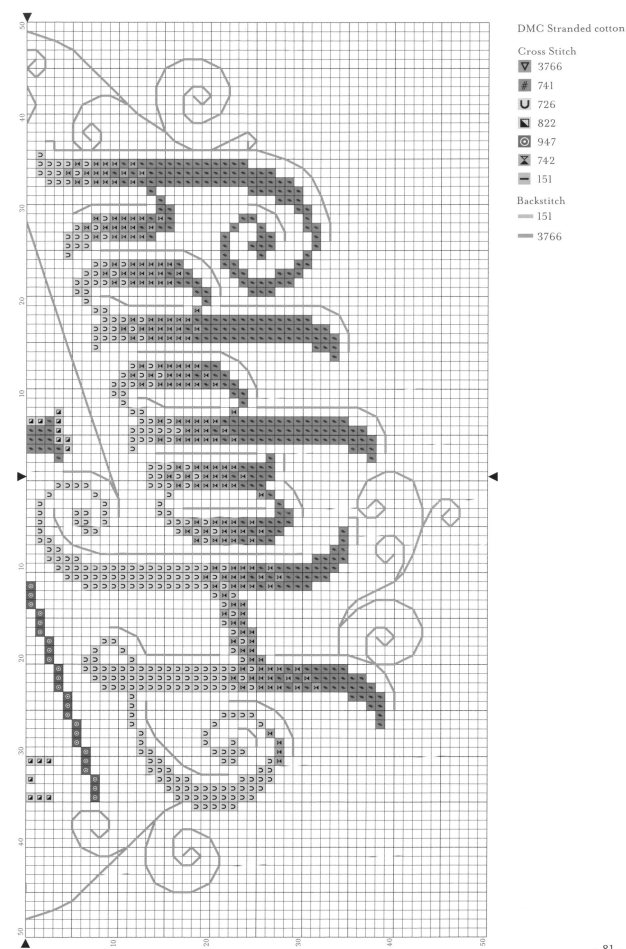

DMC Stranded cotton

Cross Stitch

▽ 3766
# 741
U 726
◧ 822
◉ 947
✕ 742
— 151

Backstitch
— 151
— 3766

very situation in life can be interpreted differently. If you seek the bad you will inevitably find it. This quote by artist Henri Matisse reminds us that it's important to have a positive mindset and be open to good things even when situations may not be promising. You never know what you'll miss if you're not looking for it.

**Info**
Stitch count: 132 x 186
Stitched size (on 14-count Aida or 28-count linen): 24 x 33.8cm (9⅝ x 13½in)

**Shopping List**
· 1 skein of each DMC stranded cotton (floss) listed in the chart key

· Ivory or Platinum Aida or linen, at least 40 x 52cm (15¾ x 20¾in)

*Model stitched by Hayley Wellock*

DMC
Stranded
cotton

Cross Stitch

| ◑ | 721 |
| • | 3828 |
| ◣ | 3819 |
| V | 581 |
| ═ | 3849 |
| ➔ | 3808 |
| S | 151 |
| ◣ | 899 |
| P | 738 |
| ╱ | 420 |
| ⌐ | 166 |
| 5 | 563 |
| ◯ | 3848 |
| ✪ | 3354 |
| ◣ | 894 |

Backstitch
━ 581
━ 166
━ 3808
━ 562

**Cross Stitch**

◑ 721
⊡ 3828
◣ 3819
V 581
≡ 3849
➡ 3808
S 151
◤ 899
P 738
╱ 420
г 166
5 563
◖ 3848
✿ 3354
◣ 894

**Backstitch**
— 581
— 166
— 3808
— 562

his timeless quote by Mother Teresa reminds us that even though not all of us have the power to do great things, it's so rewarding doing the small things with all of our heart and passion. Only you know what makes you truly feel happy and content. Whether it's making a birthday cake for a loved one or taking the dog for a walk, these little tasks can bring immense pleasure.

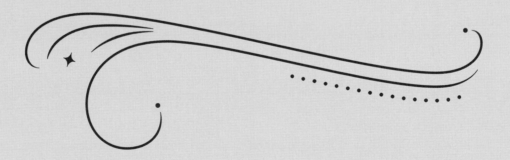

### Info
Stitch count: 97 x 97
Stitched size (on 14-count Aida or 28-count linen): 17.6 x 17.6cm (7 x 7in)

### Shopping List
- 1 skein of each DMC stranded cotton (floss) listed in the chart key

- Ivory Aida or linen, at least 34 x 34cm (13½ x 13½in)

*Model stitched by Michelle Luscombe*

Do small things with GREAT Love

MOTHER Teresa

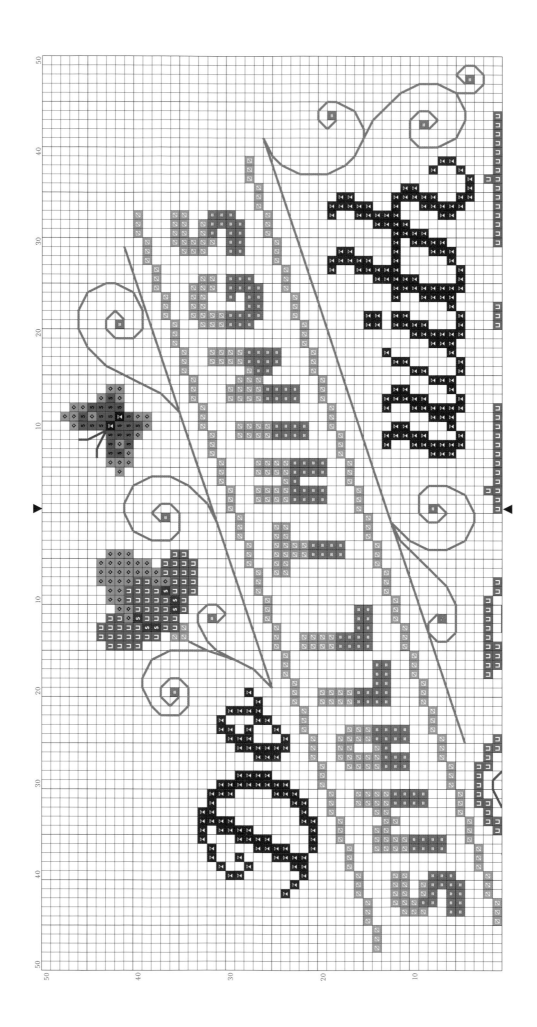

DMC Stranded cotton

Cross Stitch

| S | 920 |
| ☑ | 166 |
| ✕ | 915 |
| ◇ | 3326 |
| ⊔ | 721 |
| = | 581 |
| 5 | 603 |

Backstitch

| ▬ | 921 |
| ▬ | 581 |

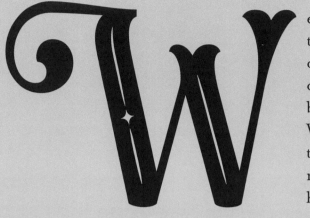

**W**e're programmed to worry – this hardwired ability has kept our species alive for thousands of years. But it's not always beneficial to us in today's world. We can waste vast amounts of time stressing over things that may never happen. Focus on the here and now in order to better enjoy today.

### Info
Stitch count: 130 x 194
Stitched size (on 14-count Aida or 28-count linen): 23.6 x 35.2cm (9⅜ x 13⅞in)

### Shopping List
- 1 skein of each DMC stranded cotton (floss) listed in the chart key, plus 1 additional skein of colour 3809

- White Aida or linen, at least 40 x 51cm (15¾ x 20⅜in)

*Model stitched by Eleanor Welsh*

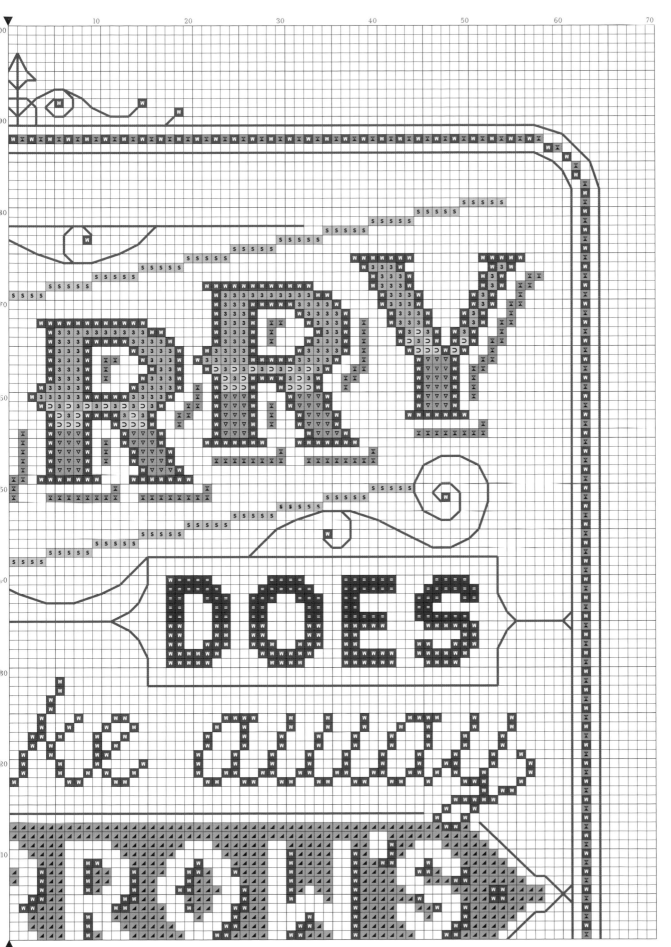

DMC
Stranded
cotton

Cross Stitch

| Symbol | Colour |
|---|---|
| ⊠ | 993 |
| S | 3811 |
| W | 3809 |
| ▽ | 471 |
| ⊃ | 10 |
| ◑ | 992 |
| ═ | 3808 |
| ◣ | 761 |
| 3 | 472 |

Backstitch
— 3809

 like to believe that the future isn't pre-determined and that ultimately no one knows what cards they'll be dealt. However, I guarantee that to worry or think anything other than positively about the future takes away from the enjoyment of today. This quote is a good one to remember if you're going through a tough patch and not feeling at your best. It serves as a reminder to hope for better days ahead.

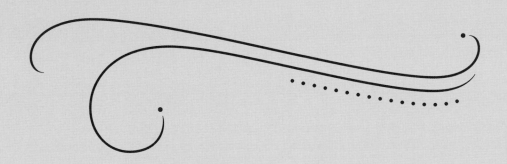

## Info
Stitch count: 98 x 97
Stitched size (on 14-count Aida or 28-count linen): 17.8 x 17.6cm (7 x 7in)

## Shopping List
- 1 skein of each DMC stranded cotton (floss) listed in the chart key

- Antique white Aida or linen, at least 33 x 33cm (13 x 13in)

*Model stitched by Michelle Luscombe*

DMC Stranded cotton

Cross Stitch

| ⊢ | 12 |
| ◕ | 34 |
| ⬆ | 958 |
| T | 3354 |
| ◖ | 3810 |
| 4 | 3823 |
| A | 818 |
| ↖ | 747 |
| ▭ | 598 |
| ◉ | 3808 |
| ⋈ | 3812 |

Backstitch

| ▬ | 3808 |
| ▬ | 34 |

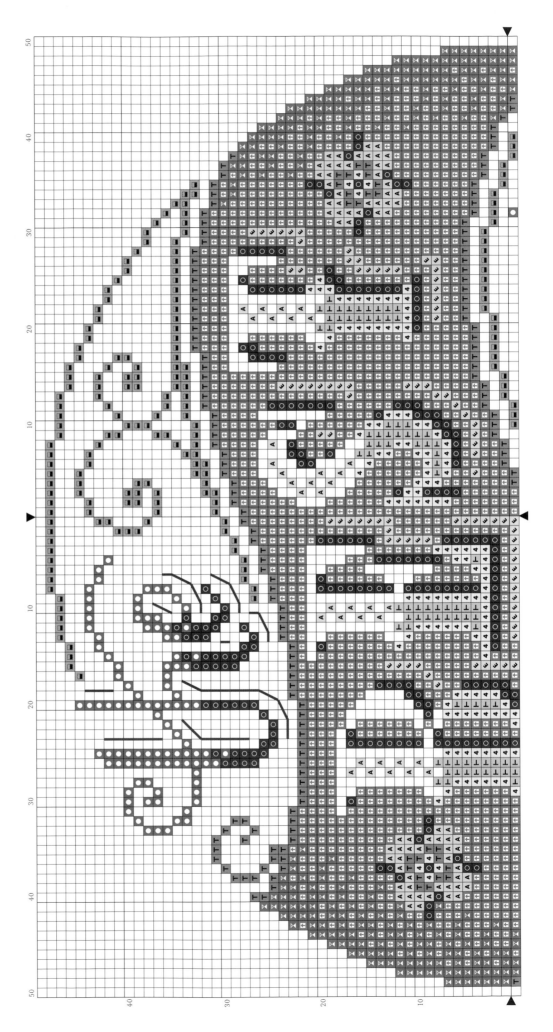

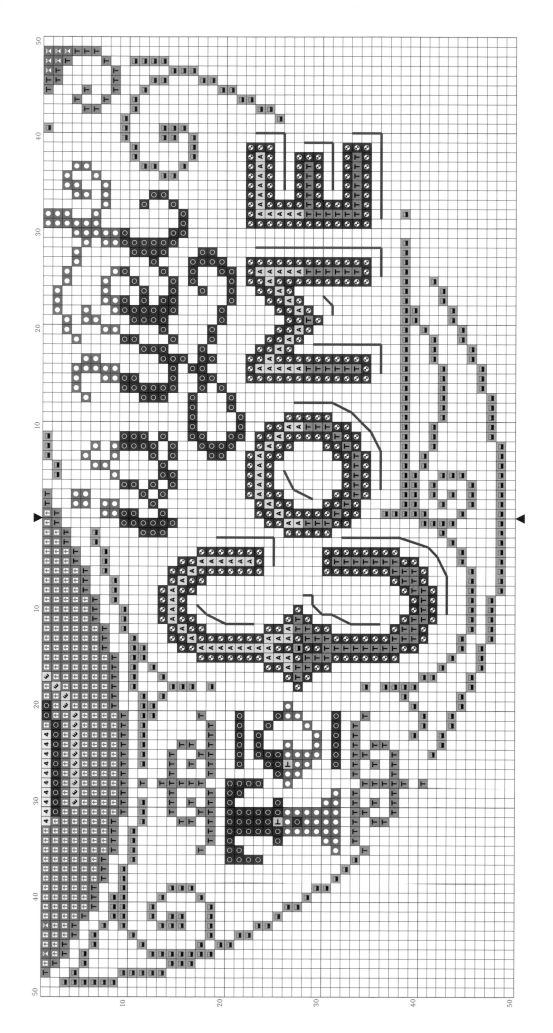

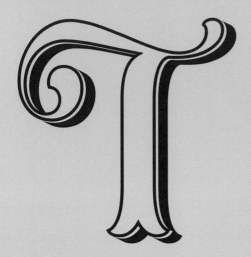

hese famous words from Nelson Mandela remind us that unless we attempt challenging things, they'll never be achieved. Even in the most difficult situations and circumstances amazing things can happen. It tells us a lot about the resilience of this extraordinary man. So, keep faith in yourself and never give up – even if you're told it's not possible.

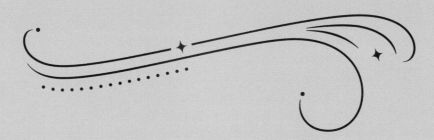

**Info**
Stitch count: 98 x 128
Stitched size (on 14-count
Aida or 28-count linen):
17.8 x 23.2cm (7 x 9⅛in)

**Shopping List**
- 1 skein of each DMC stranded cotton (floss) listed in the chart key

- Navy Aida or linen, at least 34 x 37cm (13½ x 14½in)

*Model stitched by Sharon Atkinson*

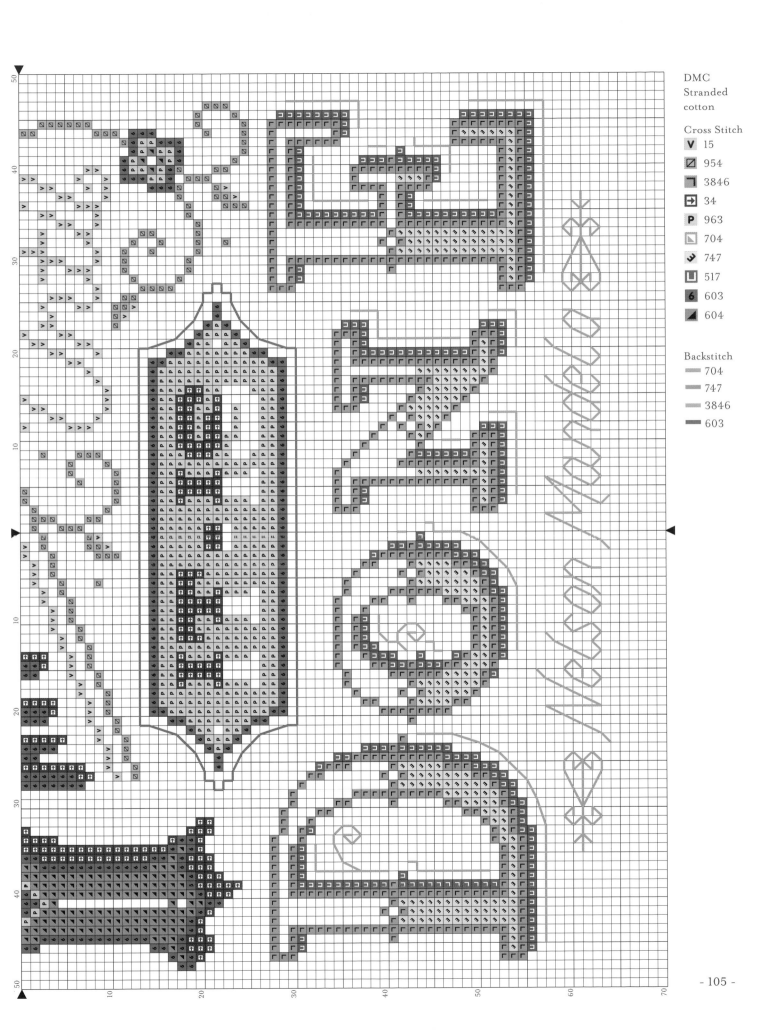

DMC
Stranded
cotton

Cross Stitch

V 15

☑ 954

◥ 3846

➔ 34

P 963

◱ 704

◞ 747

⊔ 517

6 603

◢ 604

Backstitch

━ 704

━ 747

━ 3846

━ 603

# Techniques

## Preparing the Fabric

Always begin by ensuring that you have a piece of fabric large enough for your design. Make sure there is a good amount of clearance around the edge to allow for framing – I recommend at least 10cm (4in) on each side. To find the centre of the Aida fabric, fold the fabric in half and then in half again. Mark the centre point with a needle.

It's rubbish getting halfway through a piece and realizing the edges of your fabric are getting all frayed and tatty. A good way to avoid this is to use a zigzag stitch on a sewing machine to keep your edges in place. If you don't have a sewing machine, fear not! Masking tape folded over all of the sides is an easy alternative. Just remember to add a little extra fabric to the area if you plan to do this, as you'll need to chop it off before washing.

## Cross Stitch

Once you've got the hang of this, the rest is a doddle! Working with two strands of thread in your needle, start your first cross stitch in the centre of the design and the centre of your fabric. You can stitch in rows by colour or individually depending on your preference (I tend to mix and match, depending on how I'm feeling).

To start, bring the needle up through the back of the fabric, leaving a 2cm (1in) tail of thread behind, which you should secure with your subsequent stitches. Take the needle back down through the fabric, creating a diagonal stitch, making sure that the thread tail at the back stays in place.

Keep doing this until you have finished a row (1), and then come back the other way, crossing the stitches diagonally to complete the row (2). Try to keep the top stitches running in the same direction if possible, as it creates a neater finish.

Continue to stitch until you have finished a section in that colour. At the end of the last cross stitch, the needle should be at the back of the fabric. Thread the needle through the back of four or five stitches to secure the thread, then cut away any excess.

Making a row of cross stitch on Aida

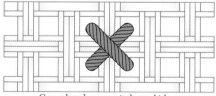

Completed cross stitch on Aida

Making a row of cross stitch on linen

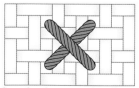

Completed cross stitch on linen

## Backstitch

This stitch is ideal for adding detail, but it can be less forgiving than cross stitch. For backstitch, you will use a single strand of thread.

To start, bring the needle up through the fabric at the point of the first stitch, leaving a 2cm (1in) tail at the back, which you should secure with your subsequent stitches. Bring the needle back through the fabric at the point where the stitch will finish to create one backstitch. Next, bring the needle up at the point where the next stitch will finish and back down through the point where the first stitch starts. Continue until all of the backstitches in the chosen area have been completed.

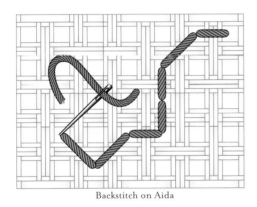

Backstitch on Aida

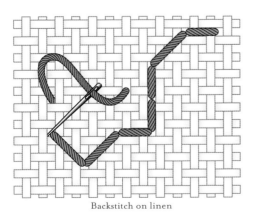

Backstitch on linen

## Stitch Count and Design Size

For each design in this book I have given the finished size and stitch count based on the type of fabric and size of weave that I have used. It is important to note that if you choose an alternative count of fabric it will change the finished design size.

To work out the size of your final design, first work out the stitch count (if it has not already been given). Do this by counting the number of stitches along the width of the design and then the number along the height. Each number should then be divided by the count of the fabric you're using in order to give you the width and height in inches.

For Aida fabric the count represents the number of threads per inch. For linen it's the same but, because you stitch over two threads rather than one, divide the count by two before making your calculations.

For example, if the finished size is given as 120 w x 140 h on 16-count fabric (or 32-count linen):

- 120 divided by 16 = $7\frac{1}{2}$in
- 140 divided by 16 = $8\frac{3}{4}$in
- The final design size is $7\frac{1}{2}$ x $8\frac{3}{4}$in.

This is as confusing as cross stitch gets, but there are plenty of calculators available online if your brain feels like it has turned to mush at this point!

## Following Charts

Cross stitch is easy to follow once you get the hang of it. The charts are made up of multiple coloured squares, each featuring symbols, which refer to a chart key. Here's a handy guide to reading charts:

- Each coloured square represents a whole cross stitch.

- The symbols relate to specific thread colours and should be cross-referenced against the key at the side of the chart.

- Single lines of colour represent backstitches or long stitches, and are also shown in thread colours highlighted in the key.

- There can also be other stitches, such as fractional cross stitches and French knots, but I haven't used them within this collection of designs, so there's no need to worry!

## Cleaning

Always hand wash your work with a delicate detergent in warm water. Do not rub or wring, but rather soak and gently agitate after a few minutes. Rinse well in cold water and allow to dry flat. I'm always terrified to wash pieces, but as long as you've used good quality branded stranded cotton and colourfast fabric you should have no issues with colours running. When you're ready to iron, place a towel on your ironing board and then iron your piece right side down over this, using a hot steam setting. *Et voila!*

## Framing

There are so many options for framing embroidery these days, so feel free to choose what works for you. I sometimes just use a simple hoop, which is laced from the back. This inexpensive method of framing is perfect for creating multiple designs for a feature wall. You can also paint the hoops or wrap them with ribbon for added pops of complementary colours.

Throughout this book I have used a few different framing options to demonstrate the various looks you can create. Take a look through the pages and choose your favourite – you may decide to replicate the method I've chosen for a particular design or to try something new.

Cross Stitch

| Symbol | Colour |
|---|---|
| ↓ | 743 |
| ♥ | 744 |
| ▽ | 3765 |
| ◖ | 967 |
| L | 3854 |

# Conversion Chart

I have used DMC thread; however, if you prefer, you can use Anchor, which is just as good. This conversion chart shows all the colours used in this book.

| DMC | Anchor | DMC | Anchor | DMC | Anchor | DMC | Anchor | DMC | Anchor |
|-----|--------|-----|--------|-----|--------|-----|--------|-----|--------|
| 09 | 1050 | 353 | 6 | 725 | 305 | 930 | 1035 | 3766 | 167 |
| 10 | 259 | 370 | 855 | 726 | 295 | 931 | 1034 | 3772 | 1007 |
| 12 | 253 | 371 | 854 | 728 | 305 | 947 | 330 | 3782 | 899 |
| 15 | 253 | 372 | 853 | 730 | 845 | 948 | 1011 | 3802 | 1019 |
| 26 | 108 | 420 | 374 | 733 | 280 | 954 | 203 | 3806 | 62 |
| 29 | 873 | 422 | 934 | 734 | 279 | 958 | 187 | 3807 | 122 |
| 30 | 118 | 433 | 358 | 738 | 361 | 963 | 73 | 3808 | 1068 |
| 31 | 119 | 444 | 290 | 741 | 304 | 964 | 185 | 3809 | 1066 |
| 33 | 92 | 445 | 288 | 742 | 303 | 967 | 1012 | 3810 | 1066 |
| 34 | 94 | 470 | 267 | 743 | 302 | 973 | 297 | 3811 | 1060 |
| 35 | 94 | 471 | 266 | 744 | 301 | 976 | 1001 | 3812 | 188 |
| 151 | 73 | 472 | 253 | 746 | 275 | 977 | 1002 | 3813 | 875 |
| 153 | 95 | 517 | 162 | 747 | 158 | 987 | 244 | 3816 | 876 |
| 155 | 1030 | 519 | 1038 | 761 | 1021 | 988 | 243 | 3817 | 875 |
| 158 | 178 | 520 | 862 | 762 | 234 | 991 | 1076 | 3819 | 253 |
| 161 | 976 | 554 | 96 | 775 | 128 | 992 | 1072 | 3821 | 305 |
| 165 | 278 | 561 | 212 | 777 | 43 | 993 | 1070 | 3823 | 386 |
| 166 | 254 | 562 | 210 | 794 | 175 | 3047 | 852 | 3825 | 323 |
| 223 | 895 | 563 | 208 | 803 | 143 | 3064 | 883 | 3828 | 373 |
| 307 | 289 | 564 | 206 | 807 | 168 | 3326 | 36 | 3836 | 90 |
| 311 | 148 | 580 | 281 | 818 | 23 | 3340 | 329 | 3839 | 176 |
| 312 | 979 | 581 | 280 | 819 | 271 | 3354 | 74 | 3840 | 117 |
| 317 | 400 | 598 | 1062 | 820 | 134 | 3608 | 86 | 3842 | 164 |
| 318 | 399 | 603 | 62 | 822 | 390 | 3609 | 85 | 3844 | 410 |
| 322 | 978 | 604 | 55 | 833 | 907 | 3706 | 33 | 3845 | 1089 |
| 333 | 110 | 608 | 332 | 834 | 874 | 3712 | 1023 | 3846 | 1090 |
| 335 | 38 | 699 | 923 | 869 | 944 | 3726 | 1018 | 3848 | 1074 |
| 336 | 150 | 702 | 239 | 890 | 218 | 3731 | 1020 | 3849 | 1070 |
| 340 | 118 | 703 | 238 | 894 | 27 | 3733 | 75 | 3854 | 313 |
| 341 | 117 | 704 | 256 | 899 | 52 | 3746 | 1030 | 3855 | 311 |
| 349 | 13 | 712 | 926 | 906 | 256 | 3755 | 939 | 3860 | 379 |
| 350 | 11 | 720 | 326 | 915 | 1029 | 3756 | 1037 | BLANC | 2 |
| 351 | 10 | 721 | 925 | 920 | 1004 | 3760 | 169 | B5200 | 1 |
| 352 | 9 | 722 | 323 | 921 | 1003 | 3765 | 170 | | |

## About the Author

Emma Congdon studied Graphic Design at the University of the Arts London. She worked as a graphic designer for advertising agencies for many years before rediscovering her love of cross stitch and becoming a freelance designer in order to pursue this passion. Her design work regularly features in magazines such as *Cross Stitcher*, *Cross Stitch Crazy* and *World of Cross Stitching*, and she has designed several pieces for DMC. This is her first book.

## Acknowledgements

Many thanks to all the hard work put in by everyone at David and Charles in the making of this book. In particular Ame Verso, for commissioning this book and all of her efforts in helping make it a reality. A special thanks to designer Sam Staddon for such beautiful layouts and to Jason Jenkins for his fabulous photography. Thanks to Jane Trollope, my editor, for all of her attention to detail, patience and care given to making sense of my words. For all their incredible hard and precise work, the stitchers involved in creating the models, Sharon Atkinson, Michelle Luscombe, Eleanor Welsh, Hayley Wellock, Glenda Dickson, Clare Prowse, Sandra Doolan and Nicola Gravener, you all blow my mind with your speed and precision and I hope you've enjoyed making these patterns as much as I've enjoyed designing them. Last but not least, thank you to my wonderful family and my partner Andy.

# Index

A DAVID AND CHARLES BOOK
© David and Charles, Ltd 2020

David and Charles is an imprint of David and Charles, Ltd
1 Emperor Way, Exeter Business Park, Exeter, EX1 3QS

Text and Designs © Emma Congdon 2020
Layout and Photography © David and Charles, Ltd 2020

First published in the UK and USA in 2020

Emma Congdon has asserted her right to be identified as author of this work in accordance
with the Copyright, Designs and Patents Act, 1988.

A catalogue record for this book is available from the British Library.

ISBN-13: 978-1-4463-0808-0 paperback
ISBN-13: 978-1-4463-7957-8 EPUB

Printed in UK by Buxton Press for:
David and Charles, Ltd
1 Emperor Way, Exeter Business Park, Exeter, EX1 3QS

10 9 8 7 6 5 4 3 2

Publishing Director: Ame Verso
Managing Editor: Jeni Hennah
Project Editor: Jane Trollope
Design Manager: Anna Wade
Design and Art Direction: Sam Staddon
Photographer: Jason Jenkins
Production Manager: Beverley Richardson

David and Charles publishes high-quality books on a wide range of subjects. For more
information visit www.davidandcharles.com.

Layout of the digital edition of this book may vary depending on reader hardware and
display settings.